Praise for Crimes of a Missed Demeanor: The Delicate Art of Effective Customer Service

"Josh Soule starts with the basics and stresses how easily the offputting question, "Can I help you?" can be transformed into a dialog with a prospective customer, which can change that initial interaction into having an active part in the customer's decision-making process."

"I was impressed by Soule's ability to see each aspect of the business experience as important, even to the cleanliness of the floors."

"I found his alternative suggestions intriguing and having the potential to turn a mildly interested visitor into a prospective buyer."

"His advice on dealing with abusive customers is refreshing and quite helpful."

"A brief text, but one that is filled with essential and note-worthy tweaks that can change your attitude towards your business and make it thrive. It's highly recommended."

Crimes of a
Missed Demeanor

The Delicate Art of Effective Customer Service

Josh Soule, MBA

Crimes of a Missed Demeanor: The Delicate Art of Effective Customer Service

First Edition: 2020

Non-Fiction: Business & Management

ISBN: 9798696968285

Contents

"When someone feels valued,
they will do more
than the expected minimum."

Introduction

The first question you are asking yourself is *"Is this book right for me?"*

Perhaps you are just starting a new job and simply want to do your best. Perhaps you have recently gotten promoted and are looking for some tips. Perhaps you have been in your field for many years, and want to stay on top of an ever-changing business world.

I can assure you, no matter what your situation, if your job requires you to interact with others, this book is right for you!

The next question you're probably going to ask is *"Who are you, and why should I listen to you?"*

In the business world I'm not much more than an MBA graduate with about a decade of experience in the retail world, and currently owns his own business. I wouldn't say I'm more qualified or experienced than so many others; in fact, there are probably a million books just like this one--each with their own unique ideas and strategies. The ideas and strategies I share come from my education, and experience, which I consider the best. I have worked under some of the finest leaders around and learned from some of the greatest mentors. The best part is, I know this stuff works because I have put it into action again and again--I have seen the results.

The final question you may have is *"What am I going to get out of this book?"*
My goal for this book is to provide current and innovative strategies in customer service. Though I center most of these around retail store-based scenarios, they can apply to any career field.

Customer service is half of the battle of your business, the other half being what you sell or provide--the quality of your product or service. We all have that restaurant or store that we enjoy, but simply don't go there because the service is terrible. You cannot effectively function with poor customer service. If you do function, it won't be to your full potential... It will at best be half.

Most of us have some knowledge and training in customer service, but a refresher course and innovative methods are what is going to help you excel in your career.

This book is best when accompanied by my customer service workshop. Speak to your manager or owner about booking an event for your business by using the "Contact" form at www.joshsoulebooks.com

Chapter 1

Let's start with a basic customer interaction. You are at your post, and a customer enters or approaches you-- what do you say? The go-to question for so many years has been "Can I help you?"

"Can I help you?"

I urge you not to say this--remove the word "help" from your holster and replace it with something else. Asking a customer if you can stop what you're doing to deal with them makes that customer feel like an inconvenience. In fact, most customers would prefer to wander around for several minutes as opposed to bothering an employee.

We combat this by creating a more inviting environment when we engage with a customer.

Here's an example:

One day I saw a customer looking at a recipe and glancing up at the aisle signs above. It didn't take a detective to see she was looking for items on her recipe card. I didn't ask if I could help. I didn't even ask what she was looking for. I simply invited myself to be a part of her experience.

"Hello," I said.

3

"Oh, hello."

"What are you cooking today?"

"It's a casserole my mother used to make."

Now I have made this a personal experience, I even glanced at the recipe and commented on how it sounded delicious. However, she still needs help, and I want to give it, so I say:

"Alright, so what else do you need to make this?"

That's it. Boom. I have offered help without making her feel like a problem. I have made her feel comfortable and created a connection with her.

She told me what else was on her list that she hadn't gotten yet, there were two items. I offered to grab an item for her and gave her directions to the other.

When she was ready to check out, I stated one final bit of icing on the cake.

"Let me know how that turns out!"

Why on earth would I say that? Because I want the customer to come back. Even more than I want her to come back, I want her to come back and specifically look for me to be working. I want her to be the store's customer, sure, but more so, I want her to be MY customer.

"I want her to be MY customer"

Almost any interaction can turn into a personal connection with a customer. Here's another good example:

You are sitting there having a personal conversation with a coworker (because work is slow). A customer approaches.

They have certainly heard you laughing. Do you get quiet when they approach and assist them like a good little robot? No, treat them like a person--better yet, treat them like a friend. Still provide great service, but there's nothing wrong with including them in the joke or conversation (assuming of course it is appropriate).

Customers would often smile at short tales of how I thought I was locked in the cooler because I didn't realize the little button opened the door. Just like the illustration above, it makes them feel part of something like their interaction is more personal than it is business.

"Their interaction is more personal than it is business"

A quick caution, however, is that you must read body language. There definitely are people that do not want you to engage with them. It's the self-checkout principle. A customer may come in knowing exactly what they want, perhaps even an item that is a bit embarrassing. They know they can get their purchase and checkout without having to talk to anyone. You running up and chatting with them, "Hello! What are we getting today? Ooh, Maxi-Pads, how interesting," is not going to make a connection, but rather drive discomfort.

In my experience, it is easy enough to look at their body language when you say hello. Do they avert their eyes and keep walking? Do they pause for a moment as if they may be interested in a brief conversation? Pay attention to the body language of who you are interacting with.

I remember an instance of having to redirect an employee who was honestly doing his best to provide good service. The problem? He was telling stories of his military days and this particular customer was visibly uncomfortable. I could look at her body language and see that she wanted to leave and had no interest in a conversation with this man, let alone about shooting and war. How he couldn't see it is still something I will never understand, but train yourself to read body language. Reading body language will help you tailor your service to better suit your customer's needs.

Remember, your goals are to have a customer want to return because they are exceptionally satisfied with their experience and to return for that reason specifically because of you.

Key Points

➢ You are not "helping" a customer, you are interacting with them

➢ Make every interaction personal and inviting

➢ Read body language, some customers don't want a personal interaction

➢ Invite customers to come back, make them feel important

Discussion Points

1. A customer enters your store and asks where greeting cards are located. You show them the greeting card section, they select one, pay for it, and leave. How can you personalize this interaction?

2. What are some examples of body language to look for in a customer who may be uncomfortable?

Chapter 2

You see a customer in a wheelchair trying to get an item from the top shelf. You see a customer carrying a baby and trying to lift a heavy item. You see a customer with a shopping list looking at signs as if they are confused. You hear a customer say "I need to go to the bathroom."

All of these things are obvious opportunities for you to step in and give a personal experience to the customer. Note I didn't say offer to help, because we aren't asking customers if we can help, we are filling a need.

"We aren't asking customers if we can help, we are filling a need"

A customer states they need to use the restroom, tell them where it is. They may already know,

9

but it takes about half of a second to say "The restrooms are up front by the soda machine." It takes just that moment to stop and create a connection with a customer. Even if they don't want help, that's okay!

The person trying to reach an item on the top shelf may say "I got it." The person looking at a recipe card may not want to share their recipe, and they may not need help finding anything. The person going to the restroom may know exactly where it is. It doesn't matter, because you are there if they need you. You didn't offer to "help", you offered to be there--you created a connection. If they ever do need something, they will likely turn to you.

Filling a need requires a bit of pride and ownership. If you are walking and you see a piece of trash on the floor, pick it up. Why? Because it's YOUR floor. It's a reflection of you and your work. You're lying to yourself if you think customers don't see that piece of trash, and they certainly see you ignore that piece of trash.

Anticipating is a bit different, it requires forethought. It requires you to see the need before you see the struggle. It's supposed to rain tonight, so make sure you have mops and wet floor signs ready. Be prepared for what's coming. You see a mom carrying a baby enter the store, there's a decent chance she may need help carrying something because she only has one free hand. I'm not saying follow her around the store, but be AWARE she may need you at some point.

By the way, this goes with managing your staff as well. One of my go-to strategies was to read the news regularly. You'd be surprised how often I would see things such as a relative of one of my employees passed away, or someone got divorced. They may not need me to talk to, which is fine, but they may need some extra time off, or an easier work assignment for a while.

Your goal is to make your staff feel as if they are valued. Just like customers. When someone feels valued, they will do more than the expected minimum.

"When someone feels valued, they will do more than the expected minimum"

I'm not saying that you need to be personally involved with your employees, in fact, I discourage it. But bear in mind that you want to have a personal CONNECTION with them. If they are thinking about quitting for another job, wouldn't you rather know in advance that they are looking, instead of when they give their notice? Absolutely.

I make it a point to catch up with my employees every day and see what's new. That's how I find that they are interested in this other career field, or their marriage is on the rocks, or they are considering college or military. All of these things affect me and how I manage--so there's an obvious business motive in addition to just being a good person and sharing a connection.

It's important to me that my staff and customers feel valued. They are important to me. They pay my bills and feed my children. For that reason, I want to provide them with the best service possible, which includes having their needs met--preferably without them having to ask.

My wife and I own a bookstore, many used bookstores don't track inventory, but we do (we will discuss this further in a later chapter). One of the many advantages of this is we can see what customers buy. So that customer working their way through a particular author or series is always pleased when we have the next book waiting for them when they come in. They didn't ask or make a special request, we just saw what was happening and responded to it.

"They didn't ask or make a special request, we just saw what was happening and responded to it"

I encourage you to stop and just watch what is happening; watch your customers, watch your staff. Stop working for five minutes and just watch--you'll be amazed at what you see.

Key Points

➤ Don't ask if you can help, just help

➤ Remember to watch body language

➤ Listen and observe for needs that can be anticipated
  o Pay attention to customers, weather, special circumstances

➤ Make customers and staff feel valued by noticing their individual needs

Discussion Points

1. List several (at least 5) needs that you can easily fill on a daily basis.

2. Name a time that you filled a need when you should have anticipated the need.

Chapter 3

Unfortunately, your best service, personal connections, anticipation, and need-filling won't stop the inevitable from happening. Conflict.

There will still be a customer who is upset, employees who don't get along, employees who don't meet expectations, and strange or bizarre encounters with customers. These things happen.

Here is my best piece of advice: Take out a pen right now, and write down the values you want to be known for. Seriously, do it. Keep it in your purse, wallet, office, or somewhere you can access it (use the discussion section at the end of this chapter if you wish).

Most of us would write things like kind, loyal, respectful, trustworthy, empathetic, responsible, integrity, and so on.

The rule is, even in the most heated and emotional moment, even when you can't stand someone anymore, NEVER violate those values. If you have chosen to be known as someone who is respectful, you must always be respectful, even when it is hard. You are the image of the values you choose to represent in the most difficult times, not the easiest. That's how people will remember you, whether customer or employee.

"You are the image of the values you choose to represent in the most difficult times, not the easiest"

Here's an example:

Years ago I was given a new position that corporate thought I would excel in. For a few different reasons, I was awful in that role. It was not where I belonged.

I will never forget my bosses sitting me down and saying something like "Josh, with seeing how careful and accurate you always are--we thought this would be a good fit for you. But it's just not your thing, so we're going to move you somewhere else."

I was told I was not cutting it, and reassigned, all in a way that was not disrespectful to me. Of course, I felt a little bad, but that was because of the situation, not the words that came from my boss. At the end of the day, I still respected him and wanted to do a good job for him.

Could he have chosen to leave me in that role, write me up, suspend me, fire me? Of course! But he chose long before this situation to be a compassionate person, he chose to mentor. He wanted me to work in my element, and therefore he would put me in a role I would succeed in.

It's no different with a customer. They may be screaming at you over the bag of apples they bought that had a rotten one. They may be swearing and spitting when they talk. It may take every fiber of your being not to shout back at them. But you chose long before them to be respectful, so you will be just that.

I should mention, I do not condone verbal abuse. There is a line that customers cannot cross, it is not fair to you or your employees to deal with customers who cross that line--no salary is high enough to be abused.

You can still be respectful when you say "I can see that you are frustrated, and I don't believe we are going to be able to have a conversation about this right now so I need you to please leave the store." Note that I didn't say the cliche phrase of "I'm going to have to ask you to leave". That's because, at that point, it's not a question--you're not asking. You need them to leave. You may even need to call the police if they refuse. They need to understand the seriousness of the situation, but in a way that you are still treating them with respect and dignity.

You don't need to take abuse, you don't need to be walked over, you can be authoritative and remain respectful and true to your values.

"You can be authoritative and remain respectful and true to your values"

The keyword to remember is boundaries. Staff and customers will learn where your boundaries are-- what will and will not be tolerated in your business. It's alright to put a stop to unacceptable behavior, in fact, it's vital to your success. It's also vital that staff and customers know where your personal boundaries are, the ones you refuse to cross--it shows your ethics.

Key Points

- ➢ Never sacrifice your values during a tense situation, this is when they are needed most

- ➢ Prompt action and respect will resolve most problems

- ➢ Set your boundaries early, and never cross them

- ➢ When someone violates a boundary, take action
  - ○ Don't be afraid to inform a customer that they need to leave, a colleague that they have gone to far, or a subordinate that their behavior is unacceptable

Discussion Points

1. What are the values you most want to be remembered for?

2. What personal boundaries can you set and apply to your current position?

3. A coworker or subordinate informs you that a customer has been talking flirtatiously with them, and the coworker expressed it makes them uncomfortable. How would you handle this situation?

Chapter 4

Top-notch customer service, superior staff, and an innovative business model cannot make up for the fact that your company is in business to make money. Therefore, the handling of money is a very important task. Not just cash, but all assets--supplies (and yes, assets include people).

Customers see the condition of your store, furniture, equipment, and product. They can certainly see the morale of staff, and the overall impression of the business. Caring for money and assets is an essential part of behind-the-scenes customer service.

I want to share with you some basic cash-handling and money-saving processes that can really help you in the long run.

Think about your non-cash assets as either one-time or recurring expenses. Your office desk would be a one-time thing (it may be replaced after a number of years of course), while paper towels in the restroom are recurring. Look around your business, there are A LOT of one-time expenses; the floors, the doors, windows, shelves, furniture, and employees. Because of the hiring expenses (not payroll), employees are an investment--you put money into background checks, drug testing, or the time invested in recruiting and onboarding, training, and so on.

"Employees are an investment"

One-time expenses should not be skimped on; get quality over a bargain price. Why? Because you want it to last forever. The other side to this is you need to take care of these assets so that they will last. Clean your desk, floors, windows, etc.-- use proper maintenance. Train and take care of your staff, make them feel appreciated and valued, don't burn them out. Stay up on the warranty and required maintenance of equipment--this is huge. Many of these more expensive items can have repairs done at no cost to you if you have complied with their warranty and routine maintenance.

YOU are an investment as well, so take care of yourself! Eat right, exercise, take that vacation--do things that are going to help you reduce stress.

Recurring expenses are where you shoot to save as much as possible, keep your monthly costs low. Buy in bulk, find services that can cut expenses for you, find cheaper alternatives. Find energy-efficient alternatives to things such as fluorescent lighting, TVs, computers, and equipment. Find a supply company to provide paper towels, toilet paper, soap, janitorial supplies, and things such as this. When possible try not to buy from a retail store unless you can get a good bulk rate.

Using rags as opposed to paper towels is a great cost-cutting item. Look around at how these recurring costs can be reduced.

One place costs should never be cut is in the quality of product or service. Quality should be an essential aspect of your business, don't think of this as a reducible expense. Reducing general expenses, however, will provide you more leeway in the core of your business sales.

Here is an illustration on quality:

We provide bags for customers who buy several items (as do most retail stores). I wince at the cost of these bags walking out the door each month. We now display hand-drawn cartoons and designs on the bags, especially for special orders; "Happy Birthday Mark!", etc. Customers love the bags, and it has become an aspect of quality service. I feel much better about the expense (by the way I couldn't get a cheaper deal, it's the best price around) knowing that it shows our quality and care.

On the other side of the fence, I poured through distributors until I found the lowest cost I could on hand soap, paper towels, etc.

I mentioned earlier that we track our inventory in our bookstore. Another reason we do this, besides customer service, is to ensure our shelves have the items customers are looking for. We track genres, authors, specific books, days, and times of the week that get high sales, and any other information I can get to ensure that when a customer enters the store - they get what they want.

I'm using this chapter as if you are the one responsible for ordering these items, if that's not the case, you still can cut costs. As I mentioned, use rags over paper towels, keep one-time items clean and well-maintained, take care of yourself and your coworkers, and do what you can to help your business last.

"Do what you can to help your business last"

What about cash? Cash is an obvious asset to the business. If your business results in direct sales to customers, you likely handle cash, checks, cards, and electronic payments. Of course, you want to handle these items with precision--double-check for accuracy with anything you do. Additionally, you want to handle these transactions as if they take second row to the customer. NEVER treat a customer as if they are less important than the money they provide!

"NEVER treat a customer as if they are less important than the money they provide"

Here are some basic tips:

When a customer pays in cash, set the cash on top of the till or counter until the transaction is complete, they have gotten their change/receipt and items, then place their money in the till. This is a pretty basic maneuver, and you likely are already doing this. It creates less of a chance for mistakes such as them saying they gave you a $10 when they only gave you a $5, but it also shows them that you care more about their experience in your store than their money. Shoving cash in a register like a greedy little goblin doesn't exactly convey quality service. Ensuring the customer is taken care of before you worry about payment makes them want to return.

When working with online, over the phone, or other types of not in-person transactions, provide the same strategy. Ensure their needs are met, they are satisfied, and everything is in order before you convey your worry about money. When we do special orders, typically the first thing I state to a customer is a price quote. They ask for a certain item, I respond with price options, then we make a transaction. In order to keep it less about money, and more about them, I provide a personal experience. Here is an example:

"Hi, do you have XYZ?"

"I'm really sorry but we don't have it in stock. However, I can place a special order for you. It would be $14.99 new or $10.99 used, both should be here in 3-5 business days and will have free shipping, do you have a preference on new or used?"

"Used is fine."

"I'll get that order placed right away for you so it gets here as soon as possible, sorry we didn't have it in stock."

"It's no problem, thank you."

"My pleasure! Is there anything else I can get for you while I'm creating your order?"

"No, that's all."

"Excellent, you should receive an order confirmation here shortly that allows you to pay. You can also pay in our store if you prefer. Thank you for letting me help you today!"

This may seem like a pretty basic customer interaction but look carefully at what has happened. There was an initial problem, but the customer was immediately offered a solution. She was also given options to better suit her needs, and I was clear about all costs and fees upfront--this is the only reason I mention money at this point, so she knows what she is getting, like the price tag on an item. After that, I make sure all of her needs are met, she is satisfied with her order, then I mention how she can pay--just like you would put the cash in the drawer after everything else is done. I am more worried about her satisfaction than I am her money.

"I am more worried about her satisfaction than I am her money"

Key Points

- ➤ Take care of investments
  - ○ Furniture, equipment, building, employees, and yourself

- ➤ Don't sacrifice quality of your product or service

- ➤ Find ways to cut small-time costs

- ➤ Make sure customers are valued above their payments

- ➤ People are your greatest investment

Discussion Points

1. What are some ways you can cut recurring costs in your current position?

2. What are some ways you can cut one-time costs in your current position?

3. What are your company's policies on freebies (for example, a customer is a few cents short at the register--do you not complete the sale, or take the shortage?) What are the limits?

Chapter 5

Unless you work for a major company or something that generates a lot of public interest, chances are you won't run into the news a lot. Customers, however, will make small talk, look around your shop, then tell everyone they know about their experience, particularly if it is a bad one. That is why customer service is essential to your business, but it is also important to be careful about harmless comments and jokes that may be misconstrued.

"Be careful about harmless comments and jokes that may be misconstrued"

Here are some tips:

Don't talk or joke about finances with customers. You aren't struggling, having a hard time, sales aren't low, and you're not worried about being able to make payroll. If you're an employee, don't talk about your salary, your bills, your child support, or anything else money-related. There is no positive outcome to this, I promise. It's one thing for your friends and family to ask how work is going, but for a stranger--there is no purpose. They will recommend your business based on the service you provide, not because you are struggling. Saying business isn't going great is equivalent to asking or begging for help, and though you may need it, people don't like being put into that position. Money related questions should be as limited as possible, "it's going well, I enjoy it."

Don't talk about anything personal, if you are asked--keep it brief. It's weird, but people get too personal with strangers. They see my wife and I run a business and ask questions about how that affects our kids or how we have any time together. It's a pretty general question, so I give a general answer; "Our kids love the store, and we have a lot of time together since we have employees who can take care of the place when we leave." Anything more than that is too much. Why is this important? Because you never know when an innocent comment can be taken the wrong way or strike a certain chord with someone.

Don't talk about forbidden material. Politics, relationships, drinking stories, or anything else that isn't about the customer's experience, or polite banter (weather, etc). I will never forget when I was just 18 years old and learning to run a cash register, a customer walked up to me, I asked how she was doing as I started to scan her items. She told me she'd be doing a lot better if XYZ politician wouldn't have signed this bill, and he's definitely the antichrist. I really didn't want to know how she was doing, I was just trying to be polite, so I started asking "did you find everything okay?" instead. Now in our store, we ask "Did you get everything you wanted?" It's a much more tactful question because it opens it up for them to talk about what they like and might get next time.

You want to be viewed as professional by customers. Professional beats friendly and casual any day of the week. Don't get me wrong, you should always be friendly--but they aren't looking for a friend - they are looking for a business interaction.

"Professional beats friendly any day of the week"

A customer trusts you to handle their money, make recommendations, and assist them in whatever services your business provides. It's hard to trust someone that is viewed as too casual. Don't get me wrong, do be friendly, but remember that it's a business and that's what the customer is hoping to find--a business, not a social club.

I saw a training video once that was very direct to never tell a customer "I don't know". I never understood that video, it makes employees feel frustrated and confused when they don't know something. I have said that at least a hundred times to customers, and never got a negative reaction. Of course, I followed it up with action: "I don't know, but let me find out and I'll call you right back." "I don't know, but let me look--I'll be right back."

I mention this because timidity doesn't convey professionalism, customers don't want you to be afraid of messing up--they want results. Customers deserve prompt action when something is wrong.

"Customers deserve prompt action when something is wrong"

Not knowing the answer to their question is a problem, and problems are going to happen. But when problems happen, SOLVE THEM. Solve them quickly and politely, apologize for the delay or inconvenience, and move on.

Key Points

- ➤ Be careful of jokes or humor

- ➤ Always be professional with colleagues and customers

- ➤ If something is wrong, action speaks louder than an apology

- ➤ Never discuss financial matters with customers

Discussion Points

1. A customer asks you a question you don't know the answer to, your supervisor has gone home for the day. What can you do?

2. A customer asks you what your thoughts are on a hot political issue (abortion, gay rights, etc). How can you respond to their question?

Chapter 6

It's not enough to "watch the training video", or attend the seminar, then get to work. What's going to make the difference in your company is action. If you remember anything from this book, remember this: It's action that creates the culture of your business, not policy.

"It's action that creates the culture of your business, not policy"

Customers will see how you behave, interact, take pride in your work. Colleagues will remember your attitude, willingness to jump in, and help. Colleagues won't say "I hated working at that place... policies were well-written though." Customers won't say "the staff there is so rude... but I'm sure their training videos were top-notch."

At the end of the day, people are going to remember how your service made them feel. It is so important to treat every interaction, even the negative ones as if you are talking to the CEO who is disguised as a customer or employee.

"At the end of the day, people are going to remember how your service made them feel"

My challenge to you is to think about the changes you want to make in your job, your department, your business. Really think about how you want customers and colleagues to see you. Then, put those changes into action!

Take small steps every day in the direction of making your store a little better. A simplified plan of action is below, use it as a reference to create your own.

Key Points

- ➢ Action speaks louder than policy

- ➢ Problems can be solved with prompt action

- ➢ Do not make your customers feel as if their problem is an inconvenience

- ➢ This book is useless without action

Sample Action Plan

Goal	Deadline	Steps
Reduce Wasted Supplies	1 Week	• Use rags instead of paper towels to clean • Use mugs instead of styrofoam cups
Increase Personalized Customer Experiences	1 Month	• Use strategies from this book • Verify effectiveness through customer surveys
Improve Employee Satisfaction	1 Month	• Create personalized experiences with employees • Make efforts to anticipate and fill employee needs • Verify through an anonymous employee survey
Update Company Values	1 Month	• Create a list of new values with employee input • Vote / mutually decide on new values • Post for all to see

Now it's your turn. It may be nothing like mine, that's okay, but make a list of changes you'd like to see in your job or company. Write those changes in the "goal" field, then write the steps to make those changes in the "steps" field, then come up with a reasonable deadline (it helps if you put a hard date instead of a loose phrase like I did).

If you have a team or subordinates, you may choose to do this activity with them instead of by yourself.

Choose to take action.

Your Action Plan

Goal	Deadline	Steps

About the Author

Josh Soule is an educator and small business owner in Fremont County, Wyoming. With a Master's Degree in Business Administration and about a decade of retail experience, he strives to continue learning and growing in a business world that is always evolving.

In conjunction with this book, Josh Soule offers a short workshop (available online or in-person depending on location) that can be requested by contacting him on his website at www.joshsoulebooks.com

* 9 7 9 8 6 9 6 9 6 8 2 8 5 *